ANIMAL TAILS
A Song about Animal Adaptations

By VITA JIMÉNEZ
Illustrations by KATY HUDSON
Music by ERIK KOSKINEN

CANTATA
LEARNING

WWW.CANTATALEARNING.COM

CANTATA
LEARNING

Published by Cantata Learning
1710 Roe Crest Drive
North Mankato, MN 56003
www.cantatalearning.com

A note to educators and librarians from the publisher: Cantata Learning has provided the following data to assist in book processing and suggested use of Cantata Learning product.

Publisher's Cataloging-in-Publication Data
Prepared by Librarian Consultant: Ann-Marie Begnaud
Library of Congress Control Number: 2016937994
    Animal Tails : A Song about Animal Adaptations
    Series: Animal World : Songs about Animal Adaptations
    By Vita Jiménez
    Illustrations by Katy Hudson
    Music by Erik Koskinen
    Summary: Full-color illustrations and music help readers discover how animals have adapted their tails for different uses.
    ISBN: 978-1-63290-765-3 (library binding/CD)
Suggested Dewey and Subject Headings:
    Dewey: E 591.4
    LCSH Subject Headings: Animals – Adaptation – Juvenile literature. | Tail – Anatomy – Juvenile literature. | Animals – Adaptation – Songs and music – Texts. | Tail – Anatomy – Songs and music – Texts. | Animals – Adaptation – Juvenile sound recordings. | Tail – Anatomy – Juvenile sound recordings.
    Sears Subject Headings: Adaptation (Biology). | Animals – Anatomy. | School songbooks. | Children's songs. | Folk music – United States.
    BISAC Subject Headings: JUVENILE NONFICTION / Science & Nature / Anatomy & Physiology. | JUVENILE NONFICTION / Music / Songbooks. | JUVENILE NONFICTION / Animals / General.

Book design and art direction: Tim Palin Creative
Editorial direction: Flat Sole Studio
Music direction: Elizabeth Draper
Music written and produced by Erik Koskinen and recorded at Real Phonic Studios

Printed in the United States of America in North Mankato, Minnesota.
122016   0339CGS17

ACCESS THE MUSIC!

SCAN CODE WITH MOBILE APP

CANTATALEARNING.COM

TIPS TO SUPPORT LITERACY AT HOME

WHY READING AND SINGING WITH YOUR CHILD IS SO IMPORTANT

Daily reading with your child leads to increased academic achievement. Music and songs, specifically rhyming songs, are a fun and easy way to build early literacy and language development. Music skills correlate significantly with both phonological awareness and reading development. Singing helps build vocabulary and speech development. And reading and appreciating music together is a wonderful way to strengthen your relationship.

READ AND SING EVERY DAY!

TIPS FOR USING CANTATA LEARNING BOOKS AND SONGS DURING YOUR DAILY STORY TIME

1. As you sing and read, point out the different words on the page that rhyme. Suggest other words that rhyme.

2. Memorize simple rhymes such as Itsy Bitsy Spider and sing them together. This encourages comprehension skills and early literacy skills.

3. Use the questions in the back of each book to guide your singing and storytelling.

4. Read the included sheet music with your child while you listen to the song. How do the music notes correlate to the words of the song?

5. Sing along on the go and at home. Access music by scanning the QR code on each Cantata book, or by using the included CD. You can also stream or download the music for free to your computer, smartphone, or mobile device.

Devoting time to daily reading shows that you are available for your child. Together, you are building language, literacy, and listening skills.

Have fun reading and singing!

Animal tails come in different shapes and sizes. And animals use their tails in different ways. Some use their tails to help them climb, **balance**, or swing. Others use their tails to **protect** themselves.

To find out more about animals and their amazing tails, turn the page and sing along!

Tails here. Tails there.
Animal tails are everywhere!

What can monkeys do with their tails?
They swing, swing, swing,
swing, swing, swing.

Tails here. Tails there.
Animal tails are everywhere!

What can whales do with their tails?

They splash, splash, splash,

splash, splash, splash.

Tails here. Tails there.
Animal tails are everywhere!

What can horses do with their tails?

They **swat**, swat, swat,

swat, swat, swat.

Tails here. Tails there.
Animal tails are everywhere!

What can scorpions do with their tails?

They sting, sting, sting,

sting, sting, sting.

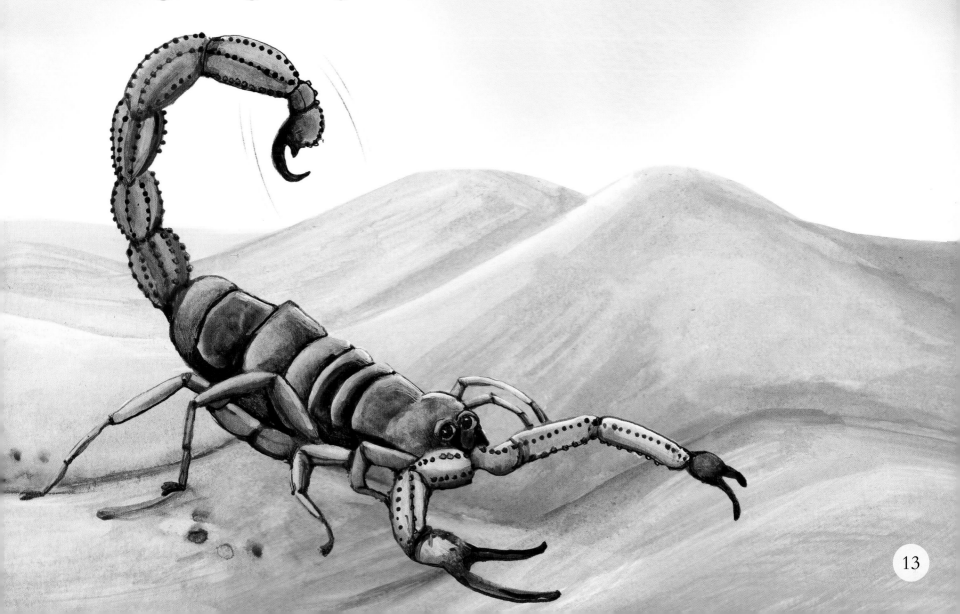

Tails here. Tails there.
Animal tails are everywhere!

What can rattlesnakes do with their tails?
They shake, shake, shake,
    shake, shake, shake.

Tails here. Tails there.
Animal tails are everywhere!

What can fish do with their tails?

They swim, swim, swim,

swim, swim, swim.

Tails here. Tails there.
Animal tails are everywhere!

What can birds do with their tails?

They **steer**, steer, steer,

steer, steer, steer.

Tails here. Tails there.
Animal tails are everywhere!

DO NOT TOUCH
THE GLASS

What can people do with their tails?

People do not have tails!

DO NOT TOUCH
THE GLASS

21

SONG LYRICS
Animal Tails

Tails here. Tails there.
Animal tails are everywhere!

What can monkeys do with their tails?
They swing, swing, swing,
  swing, swing, swing.

Tails here. Tails there.
Animal tails are everywhere!

What can whales do with their tails?
They splash, splash, splash,
  splash, splash, splash.

Tails here. Tails there.
Animal tails are everywhere!

What can horses do with their tails?
They swat, swat, swat,
  swat, swat, swat.

Tails here. Tails there.
Animal tails are everywhere!

What can scorpions do with their tails?
They sting, sting, sting,
  sting, sting, sting.

Tails here. Tails there.
Animal tails are everywhere!

What can rattlesnakes do with their tails?
They shake, shake, shake,
  shake, shake, shake.

Tails here. Tails there.
Animal tails are everywhere!

What can fish do with their tails?
They swim, swim, swim,
  swim, swim, swim.

Tails here. Tails there.
Animal tails are everywhere!

What can birds do with their tails?
They steer, steer, steer,
  steer, steer, steer.

Tails here. Tails there.
Animal tails are everywhere!

What can people do with their tails?
People do not have tails!

Animal Tails

Americana
Erik Koskinen

Refrain

Tails here. Tails there. An-i-mal tails are eve-ry-where!

Verse

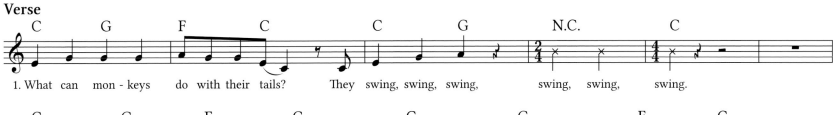

1. What can mon-keys do with their tails? They swing, swing, swing, swing, swing, swing.

Refrain

Verse 2
What can whales do with their tails?
They splash, splash, splash,
    splash, splash, splash.

Refrain

Verse 3
What can horses do with their tails?
They swat, swat, swat,
    swat, swat, swat.

Refrain

Verse 4
What can scorpions do with their tails?
They sting, sting, sting,
    sting, sting, sting.

Refrain

Verse 5
What can rattlesnakes do with their tails?
They shake, shake, shake,
    shake, shake, shake.

Refrain

Verse 6
What can fish do with their tails?
They swim, swim, swim,
    swim, swim, swim.

Refrain

Verse 7
What can birds do with their tails?
They steer, steer, steer,
    steer, steer, steer.

Refrain

Verse 8
What can people do with their tails?
People do not have tails!

GLOSSARY

balance—to keep steady and not fall over

protect—to keep safe

steer—to move in a certain direction

swat—to hit with a quick, sharp blow

GUIDED READING ACTIVITIES

1. Pick one of the animals in this book. Describe what its tail looks like. How does the shape, size, and features of its tail help the animal?

2. What kinds of animals live near you? How do those animals use their tails?

3. If you had a tail, how would you use it? Draw a picture of you using your tail.

TO LEARN MORE

Calhoun, Kelly. *Twisty Tails*. Ann Arbor, MI: Cherry Lake Publishing, 2016.

Hulbert, Laura. *Who Has This Tail?* New York: Henry Holt, 2012.

Lewis, Clare. *Mammal Body Parts*. Chicago: Heinemann Raintree, 2016.

Pearson, Carrie. *A Warm Winter Tail.* Mt. Pleasant, SC: Sylvan Dell, 2012.